Meeting To Order

HOW TO CALL A MEETING WITH YOURSELF

"Daily Success Habits That Produce Stunning Results"

CUBIE DAVIS KING

Web address: www.goldcrowninc.com
First Edition
First Printing 2003

In the U.S. write
Cubie Davis King
c/o Gold Crown Enterprises, Inc.
7046 Broadway #356
Lemon Grove, CA 91945
toll Free: 800-483-1255

Make Your Dreams King™
I'M Working On My Dream™
Mind Stamping™
Focused Believing™
Are all trademarks of
Cubie Davis King • San Diego • Dallas • New Jersey

©Copyright 2003 Cubie Davis King, All rights reserved.

No portion of How To Call A Meeting With Yourself may be
Reproduced in whole or in part without the express
Written permission of Cubie Davis King.

Published by WP Publishing
Graphics & Printing by Workin Perkins
www.workinperkins.com

How to Get the Most From This Book!

Find a quiet place and time to read and study these principles.

Read and re-read this book a minimum of five times. Repetition is the key to effective learning.

Choose one principle to study for 15 minutes each day, preferably the same one on the same day each week, e.g. Monday is my day to master goal setting, etc.

Keep a note pad by your nightstand, and keep records of all your thoughts and successes.

Finally, believe you can win.

Dedication

This book is dedicated to everyone who has ever been told to…"give up on your dreams," "it won't work," "you cant do it," and other hurtful dream killing comments.

I say to you "don't ever give up and don't ever quit. Dream your biggest dream and step into your future.

Also dedicated in loving memory of the greatest parents anyone could ask for, Sam Davis & Jewel Dean King who worked extremely hard to raise ten children and taught us to believe in ourselves. Forever love…

- Cubie Davis King

TABLE OF CONTENTS

Introduction 2

Chapter 1: *You Were Born To Win* 6

Chapter 2: *Remember This Secret* 10

Chapter 3: *What Happened To Your Dreams?* 12

Chapter 4: *What Do The Winners Do?* 16

Chapter 5: *Time to Call a Meeting with Yourself* 18

Chapter 6: *Day One: Understanding Your Life's Purpose* 22

Chapter 7: *The Secret Revealed* 26

Chapter 8: *Day Two: Become a Master at Goals Setting* 30

Chapter 9: *This is How They Do It* 32

Chapter 10: *The Powerful Goals Setting Workshop* 36

Chapter 11: *Day Three: How To Boss Your Thoughts* 42

Chapter 12: *Brace Yourself For This One* 48

Chapter 13: *Day Four: The Science Called Focused Believing*™ ..52

Chapter 14: *One Lethal Weapon* 54

Chapter 15: *Day Five: Building Unstoppable Self Confidence* 62

Chapter 16: *How Do I Change?* 66

Chapter 17: *One Rich Man* 68

Chapter 18: *Meeting Adjourned* 72

"In every battle there is a fifteen minute period when the decision can go either way. The general who knows that period and throws everything he has into the battle will win. But the general who does not know it or who is too cautious that he will not commit his reserves will lose not only the battle, but inevitably he will lose the war." —Napoleon

Introductrion

People, who lack the understanding and skills of how to succeed in life, attribute the success of others to luck.

Success has nothing to do with luck but, if you must attribute it to luck, consider this, someone said, "The harder I work the luckier I get."

Your Success depends on what you do each and every day.

And, if you feel that you've failed in the past, I have some really exciting news for you.

Are you ready? Here it is…you can actually re-program your mind to achieve stunning success in just fifteen minutes a day. You heard me right; in just fifteen minutes a day you can turn your whole life around and experience extraordinary results.

Napoleon, who was considered one of the greatest military commanders of all times, identified it as "the fifteen minute period." He said and I quote, *"In every battle there is a fifteen minute period when the decision can go either way. The general who knows that period and throws everything he has into the battle will win. But the general who does not know it or who is too cautious that he will not commit his reserves will lose not only the battle, but inevitably he will lose the war."*

We all face these crucial fifteen minute periods everyday. But make no mistake; there is a very clear distinction between those who win their daily battles and those who don't.

One Burning Question!

Ever since I can remember, even as a child, born in the projects of East Dallas, there was one burning question I promised myself I'd find the answer to in my lifetime.

The question continued to burn in my thoughts through grade school, high school, and my early military career. I was determined to find the answer to this puzzling question.

What is the question you ask? Well, here it is. I wanted to find out…what makes successful people succeed?

What makes some people do and others don't, why some people will while others won't? What makes some people studs and others duds?

My quest has taken me on an incredible forty-year journey.

During this time I've read hundreds of books, thousands of newspaper and magazine articles, attended countless success seminars, and talked to tons of successful people.

My quest has taken me all over the world and allowed me to meet people of all races, colors, and creeds.

As a young sailor, when my ship docked at various ports in Italy, Spain, France, Portugal, Holland, the Netherlands, England, and many others, I found myself drawn to shop owners to talk about success.

I found The Answer!

After many years of personal research I finally found the answer to this burning question.

The success principles I discovered, which you will find in this book, have drastically changed my entire life.

They are the exact ones that have made millionaires out of paupers, winners out of losers, and superstars out of failures. If you would follow these time-tested principles you too would succeed far beyond your wildest dreams.

Pay Close Attention

You must pay very close attention to each and every principle, because applying one without the other will not yield for you the desired results. Are you ready? Then get set, because on the following pages you'll find your golden "keys to the kingdom."

The Symbol

Whenever you're parked at a parking meter, the time left on that meter dominates your thoughts. No matter what you're doing, it's constantly on your mind.

This meter serves as a reminder that if you'd take possession of just 15-minutes a day and dedicate that crucial time to the principles of success outlined in this book, your life will change dramatically, and you'll succeed far beyond your wildest imagination. Remember just 15 minutes a day.

Try it and see for yourself.

Chapter One

You Were Born To Win!

You have an emergency phone call? As you race to the phone, your heart is pounding as if to beat right out of your chest. "O Lord, what could it be? Was there a terrible accident? Is it my husband/wife? Are my children OK? Did my house burn to the ground? Is there a death in the family?" A thousand things run through your mind in a span of a few seconds. As you quickly pick-up the phone, you take one last deep breath. "O God," (your mind whispers to the heavens), "please let everything be all right."

The voice on the other end is calm but direct. "Mr. or Ms._____?" "Yes," you answer. "I must inform you that you've just won $850 million dollars."

Your fears turn to jubilation. You can't believe it. "Me, you say, the kid who came from the other side of the tracks. The kid who was told you'll never be anything. That kid who people laughed at in school?"

It takes awhile but it all begins to sink in. You start to yell, then scream! "I'M RICH, I'M RICH!"

HOW TO CALL A MEETING WITH YOURSELF

By this time you can't think of anything else. You rush to your boss and tell him, "I'm taking the rest of the day off." "I may or may not be back, I'll call you." You walk out of the building and the sun is the brightest you've ever seen. The birds are singing and calling your name. Everyone you meet has a smile on his or her face. You can't believe it. Then, you ask yourself, "Am I dreaming?"

Well, yes you are dreaming!

Wake Up and Smell the Coffee!

Folks, for 99.99% of the people in the world, life just doesn't work that way. I think all of us at one time or another have dreamed of getting that phone call or that knock on the door. Boy, what we could do with all that money!

Sad fact is most people go through life living this type of a pipe dream. They spend their whole life hoping for one big event to happen to them. That one swing which will knock the ball out of the ballpark and win the game.

The last basket at the buzzer that will win the game and ensure their place in history. That one hidden treasure found at a garage sale that will make them rich.

Folks wake up and smell the coffee! 99.99% of the time life just doesn't work that way.

Life Will Give You What You'll Fight For

If you're going to win in this life, you have to fight for what you want. Life is a struggle and in order to win you must do battle everyday of your life. I found out life will give you what you're willing to fight for. Life will turn out the way you plan. If you settle for having money problems, that's what life will give you. If you settle for being unhappy that's what you'll get. But if you want to win, I mean really win, God will bring all the elements of heaven together to make it happen for you.

Whatever You're Looking for is Looking for You!

It's a fact. Whatever you're looking for is looking for you.

It's called the law of attraction and it works like this.

If you're looking for trouble, trouble is looking for you. If you're looking for misery, misery is looking for you (Oh, and by the way it loves company).

But if you're looking for happiness, fulfillment, and success guess what? It's already looking for you.

So thoughts become things, pure and simple. If you grasp this concept, it will bring you wealth beyond your wildest imagination.

You Choose and It Is So

The river of life is neutral. It doesn't care where you come from. It doesn't care what you look like. It doesn't even care how much money you have. It's neutral. The river just keeps flowing.

Now you can come to the river and drink of its icy cold fresh spring water anytime. You can use your hand, but don't curse the one who uses a cup. You can use a cup, but don't curse the one who uses a pitcher. You can use a pitcher, but don't curse the one who comes with a barrel. You can use a barrel, but don't curse the one who uses a drum and then decides to sell bottled water to other thirsty souls. The choice is yours and yours alone.

"Success Is Not For The Masses,

But For Those Faithful Few

Who Persevere

Till Their Dreams Become A Reality"

Chapter Two

Remember This Secret

There is something you must always remember in pursuing your dreams. Whatever you curse in life, will in turn curse you. If you curse the success of others, success (true success) will always evade you.

That statement is so powerful it may take a few days for you to digest it.

Read it over and over again until it sinks in. True winners are those who can get excited about others' success. A good speaker enjoys a good speaker.

A good doctor admires the work of a good doctor. A person who succeeds applauds the success of others.

Let me ask You a Soul Searching Question …

Is Your Dream Dead?

Remember when you were in grade school. For most of us those were happy days. We were protected from all the evils in the world.

We played on the playground freely, brought our lunch to school and traded with our friends, and we were hugged and kissed everyday. Our parents and teachers made a big fuss over us. At that age we believed we could do anything and be anything. The world was ours simply for the asking.

I remember Ms. Brooks, my second grade teacher, going around the room asking each of us what we wanted to be in life. "A fireman," one said. "A doctor," said another. "I'm going to be an actor," one stated, while still another proclaimed, "I'm going to travel the world." Each of us had a dream, whether it was to go to the NFL, the NBA, play in a BAND, become a MODEL or MOVIE STAR, remember?

We dreamed big dreams and no one was going to stop us from achieving our goals.

So we played in marching bands, tried out for cheerleader, played football, won science fairs, and yelled at pep rallies. We were excited about life!

What Happened to Your Dreams?

Do you remember those feelings you got at the pep rallies and Friday night football games? It was electrifying.

Our parents told us we looked good. Our teachers told us we looked good and even our friends told us we looked good. We were self-assured because we had high hopes and dreams.

By the time we graduated from high school, we were pumped up. We got excited about being on our own because finally our dreams would be fulfilled.

The Sad Truth

But something happened on the way to reaching our goals. We found out the world was not as kind and supportive of our dreams. When we finally reached corporate America, we got some hard lesson in reality. We found it to be a mean, dog eat dog, watch your back environment.

Companies began to take advantage of us. We found ourselves working long hours for little pay. We were playing in a game we were ill equipped to play. All of a sudden what was fun became drudgery.

The American dream of home ownership, college money for our kids, traveling the world on exotic vacations was eroding. So too was our idea of being the big boss and making a lot of money.

So with each passing year we lowered our sites a little more.

"Maybe it wasn't meant to be," we reasoned. "I really didn't want that position anyway," we sigh. "We can do without all that stuff." "We don't need a vacation." "Ah, the car is just fine." We begin to settle for far less than we ever expected.

It's Been Beaten out of You

Now when an opportunity presents itself and we attempt to get our dream back, our relatives, friends, and neighbors (as well meaning as they are), come with their negative input.

"You start a business? You've got to be kidding." Nobody has ever made it big in this family, what makes you think you're so special." "You're not smart enough." "You don't have enough education." "Where are you going to get the money?" "You better not give up that good job." Talk. Talk. Talk.

Toxic talk from toxic people.

If That's Not Enough...

Then that little voice in your head starts talking. "You know they're right." "You're not pretty enough, you didn't graduate from Harvard, you didn't come from the right side of the track, and you're not a leader. Just face it you'll be working for somebody else the rest of your life!"

As if your friends and relatives were not enough to discourage you, now that voice in your head is against you. You just can't win. The world has beaten your dreams out of you.

But you know what?

You Were Born to Win!

That's not just idle talk. You were not put here to just pass some time then die. I believe you were put here for a reason. There's a purpose for your life. Find that purpose and it's there you will find your riches.

Folks, go back to your original dreams. Yea, those dreams. The ones so many of you have given up on. I believe those original dreams of yours yet live. I believe you were made to conquer and not be conquered.

YOU WERE BORN TO WIN AND NOT LOSE!

How Bad Do You Want It?

God has put in the human spirit the ability to bounce back from adversity. Now no one is going to make you win, but winning is an option open to all of us.

Want to know another secret? You must want to win as bad as you want your next breath.

Think for a moment, every team, who has ever won the superbowl, did so because they wanted it more than the other team. In fact, they wanted it so bad they could taste it. They believed they could win. They believed it was possible.

No Fluff

You say, "That sounds like a lot of fluff to me. You're just trying to make me feel good." Well, when I tell my story it doesn't matter how you feel, I know it's true.

You see, in 1989, after many years of hard work, I lost every single thing I owned in this life. My job, my house, my two cars, my condo, everything.

I was married with three small children. All we had left was the clothes on our backs. I can't begin to tell you how devastating this was for me. I had to look in the eyes of my family who was looking to me for answers.

All kinds of questions ran through my mind. What went wrong? What could I have done differently? Did I trust the wrong people? Where were all my friends now? What are my relatives thinking and how do they view me now? Can I bounce back? There were a thousand questions for which I had no immediate answers.

Decide to Win

After weeks of walking, pondering, thinking, yes and even a little crying I had to make a gut wrenching decision. Either I was going to suck it up and make life give back all I'd lost and more, or life would deal me a fatal blow.

Everything I've studied about winning over all those years would now be tested. It was show time! After weeks of being depressed and ashamed (for putting my family through this) I decided to win. I decided not to be bullied around by the circumstances of life. I decided to be somebody.

Think and Grow Rich

Can you extract one key ingredient to my amazing and stunning turn around?

You've read it already and you'll read it again and again as you turn page after page. When it hits you take a note pad and pencil and record the date for it will mark a major turning point in your own life.

CHAPTER Four

What Do the Winners Do?

Winners do whatever it takes to win and as Art Williams said, "...and a little bit more."

One night I heard Ross Perot say on Larry King Live, that if he lost everything he had, he would get up the next day and cut lawns to feed his family.

I too decided my family would not starve, and that we would one day be on top again. At my lowest point I was looking in stinky trash dumpsters (yes, I actually climbed inside) to collect aluminum cans as a means to feed my family.

My friends didn't want anything to do with me, and some of my relatives were ashamed of me. Yes, it was embarrassing but a winner does whatever it takes to win. I was a winner even at my lowest state. You see, you'll find throughout the pages of this book that success is a state of the mind.

What do the winners do? Whatever it takes and a little bit more. Even though I was down and out, I refused to lose.

Many see me now looking all fine and say they want that same kind of success. I ask a simple question, "Can you drink of the bitter cup life will require you to sip from many times before you succeed?

But remember it's only a test. Success tests everyone who asks for the prize. Hang in there and don't ever give up.

Your Word Is Law

Speak your word long enough and it becomes law. Your words are powerful. They can produce either life or death. Scripture says that death and life are in the power of the tough.

Death words that kill the human spirit are words like, I can't, I won't ever, people like me never, and others. Speak these words long enough and they become law. They will kill your creative spirit.

Living words have a can do spirit attached to them. I can, I will, I shall! So be careful what you speak. The entire universe will support you and your words. Whether for good or for bad.

How many success keys have you picked up so far? They are in here and they will (when applied) produce stunning results.

Time to Call a Meeting with Yourself

Now get ready as I reveal some great universal truths. On the following pages you will learn some of my most jealously guarded secrets to winning in life. Secrets that truly transformed my habits of failure into habits of success.

You'll learn a very potent five-day formula that will also transform you into a powerful force for success.

In just fifteen minutes a day you will go from thinking thoughts of failure to thinking thoughts of success.

The success system that you'll find on the following pages has been proven time and again by the most successful people the world has ever known.

Are you ready to call a meeting with the one person who can change your life forever? The person who looks at you every single time you look in the mirror and the one person who knows you better than anyone else on this earth. Yes, the person who knows every thought you think and every move you make. That person is YOU!

HOW TO CALL A MEETING WITH YOURSELF

- The public you
- The private you
- The confident you
- The shy you
- The scared you
- The angry you
- The happy you
- The disappointed you
- The party you
- The stay at home you
- The skinny you
- The fat you
- The sick you
- The healthy you
- The lazy you
- The exercise you
- The up you
- The down you
- The rich you
- The poor you
- The church you
- The picnic you
- The work you

- The vacation you
- The travel you
- The mom you
- The dad you
- The friend you
- The in-law you
- The sister you
- The brother you
- The professional you
- The business you

And all the other you(s) inside of you that only you know.

Time to Set a New Course

It's time to call a meeting with yourself. It's time to bring all the you(s) in and sit them down in a round table discussion. It's high time you set them on a new course that'll move all of them in the same direction, the direction of success. Not just any success, but the kind of success that will absolutely stun others.

When you engage the success system on the following pages, you'll notice a stark difference in the way you walk, the way you talk, yes and the way you think.

You'll notice your tolerance for failure in yourself and the people who surround you will diminish significantly.

Your new appetite for success, and success minded people will rise sharply and you'll forever be changed for the better. You'll demand that life give you what you're fighting for and it will.

The success system revealed on the following pages is no fly-by-night, get-rich-quick scheme. No, it has taken me over twenty-five years to develop and perfect this system. Yet it's quick and easy to understand.

You say, "I've heard it all before." Not like this, you haven't.

Are you ready to call that meeting with yourself and win? Then get set and let's get started on day one and your first life transforming fifteen minute session. Get ready to Win!

Day One

Invest 15 Minutes Today Understanding Your Life's Purpose

Today, your 15-minute assignment that'll lead you to stunning success is to thoroughly understand your purpose in life. People who experience stunning success are people who've discovered their God given talents and are masters at marketing them. They've found that one commodity in life that allows them to be dynamic, enthusiastic, and vibrantly alive.

You too must have a definite purpose in life, and the greater that purpose the more likely you are to succeed.

How Will You Know?

People often ask the question, "How can I know, for sure, my purpose for being here or what should I be doing with my life?"

Well, there is a simple question you can ask yourself.

But first, realize the decision as to what to do with your life is yours.

The scripture says that you shall decree (or decide) a thing, and it shall be established for you, and as you go, the light will shine upon your path.

Too often unsuccessful people have this warped view that somehow God keeps them humble by making them unhappy. And that He wants them doing something in life that makes them unhappy, unfulfilled, and therefore unsuccessful.

Wrong. Wrong. Dead Wrong!

I believe with all my heart you were born to win, and there's a specific job or mission you were sent here to do.

Finding that purpose is key to your success and happiness.

Their Approach Is Backwards

The problem is many people's approach to life is backwards. They find an occupation that'll pay them the amount of money they'd like to make, but give little or no thought whatsoever as to how much or how long they'd love working in that particular field or occupation.

Soon they burn out and go on to another job and another and another.

They go through life wondering why they're never happy and never fulfilled on their jobs.

True enough they've made everyone else happy. Their moms, their dads, their coaches, their teachers, their spouses, even their in-laws because they have done what everyone else wanted them to do.

They bought into the old adage; get a good education, so you can get a good job with good benefits, and stay there, period.

If this is what you believe, then being happy and fulfilled on your job is irrelevant.

I believe that's why we see so many people who either hate their job, hate their boss, or hate their opportunity.

"If you really want the success that stuns others, you've got to follow your own heart. Do what makes you whole."

CHAPTER Seven

The Secret Revealed

Want to know the secret? Here it is: Where your heart is, that's where you'll find your treasure (or riches).

Now, re-read that statement. Now carve it in the palm of your hand.

Listen…if you'd get busy doing what makes your heart happy instead of what makes your pocketbook happy, you'd never have to worry about money ever again in your life.

It's one of the laws of the universe that clearly states, "whatsoever you sow, that's what you'll reap." Folks, sow into the lives of others, and into your life others will sow. By doing this, you'll end up reaping a harvest so abundant it'll scare you.

You see, those who experience stunning success have learned to serve others with their God given talents. If you want to become great at whatever it is that you do, then, use your talent in service to others.

Case in point…

For years I wanted to be a paid professional speaker. I tried everything to get noticed and to get speaking engagements but to no avail. It wasn't until I volunteered my time (service) to speak to others about success that my career took off.

Within four months of volunteering my time (going into middle schools sharing my knowledge and experience with young people), I was hired to travel and speak professionally.

What Would You Do?

Now, let me ask you that question.

If you could do anything you wanted with your life. If you woke up tomorrow and for whatever reason, money was no longer an object to what you really wanted to do in life.

If all your bills were paid and you no longer had to worry about the house payment, automobile payment, gas, lights, water or any other bills, and you were free every single day to do whatever you wanted with your life…what would you do?

Think about it. Think about it long and hard…

Why? Because everything you've ever dreamed of concerning success, not just any kind of success, but good success, the kind of success that comes with true happiness…everything you've ever dreamed of will be found in your answer.

It's sad, but many people consider themselves successful, but they are not truly happy.

I say, "If you are not happy you are not truly successful, no matter how much material wealth you accumulate."

So think, think long and hard about this question, and remember, whatever you decide to do with your life, if it's positive, and lifts others, and if those who watch you are inspired to be their best, then there's a very strong possibility that is your life's calling.

This is what you should be doing with your life.

Put Your Heart into It

Now, once you find your true purpose in life, when you are allowed to take your talents and use them in service to others, do it with all your heart, all your soul, all your mind, and all your might. Be the very best at what you do, and become the one whom others proudly call on for answers.

It has been said so often that if you'd help enough people get what they want out of life, you'd eventually get what you want.

When you've found your true purpose for being, you'll discover that the power of the entire universe will assist you in succeeding beyond your wildest imagination.

Any company, any organization, and any person who will be great must first learn to serve others and serve them from their heart. It's another proven law of the universe.

You've Arrived

How will you know you've arrived? Here's how…when you can get up every morning with an insatiable passion for living. When that excitement is easily detected in the way you walk, in the way you talk, and in the way you carry yourself.

When you can honestly say, "If I wasn't paid a penny to do what I'm doing, I'd yet do it for the sure passion of it, because I truly love what I do."

It's then, at that moment, you'll know beyond a shadow of a doubt that you've found your life's purpose. Then my friend you've arrived.

Day Two

I'm almost bursting with joy at revealing to you the next life skill you'll employ in your new success system. A skill that'll take you from the bottom of the totem poll to the top. The very skill that has made countless millionaires out of ordinary people just like you. It is potent.

Are you ready? Then turn the page...

Feast your eyes on this, and remember to...

Follow Your Heart...

For Where Your Heart Is

There You'll Find Your Riches

> ### Stunning Success Habit-#1
>
> Today, spend 15 minutes understanding your Life's Purpose.
>
> Do you truly love your job or occupation? If the answer is no, then have the courage to do what 90% of other people will not do...change, and you'll be rewarded with stunning success.
>
> If you are happy, then re-dedicate yourself to being the very best at what you do. Be thankful for the privilege to share your talents, knowing without a doubt, that as you serve others, the success you truly desire will in time be yours.

Chapter Eight

Day Two

Invest Fifteen Minutes Today Becoming a Master at Goals Setting

Stunningly successful people are masters at setting goals. If you could glance at the daily planners of this select group, you'd find what appears to be an art form. Each and every day they review their goals and spend time in their dreams.

They have superior knowledge of the fact that nothing becomes a reality in life until it first becomes specific. The holy writ says, "Write the vision and make it plain."

It's not enough to simply desire the things you want to achieve in life.

You must develop a specific plan and a specific deadline for their attainment.

You must crystallize your thinking and plan your steps carefully, day by day, month by month, and year by year.

Then you must become a tenacious crusader, and pursue your dreams with dogged determination, sustained effort, and supreme confidence in your ability to win.

All who experience stunning success understand that in order to be truly effective, your goals have to be in writing.

And remember this; no one becomes truly successful without first planning to do so.

When you set meaningful goals, you're in essence creating your own future.

This Is How They Do It

Here's how the highly successful do it. They start with an overall goal for their life. They have a dream of where they want to be by a certain age (say age 55). They get that picture crystal clear in their minds, then, it's reduced to writing. It may read like this:

You Create Your Own Future

I _____, in exchange for the talents given me in this life, will spend my days working in service to others as a _____.

I have total confidence that as I serve others, my life will be rich and full. I will retire without any fears, including a shortage of money or any other thing at the age of _____.

You see, master goals setters chop their big dreams into little goals.

They plan where they want to be in say, 20 years, 15 years, 10 years, 5 years, and 3 years.

"To Do" List Must Serve a Purpose

Then they go to work on their yearly goals, breaking them down into the four quarters of the year.

They break them down further into weekly goals and finally into daily "to do" list.

Take note: This is one of the greatest skills you'll ever learn.

I can almost guarantee, those who have never learned to employ these skills, never experience the success they truly desire and deserve.

Do you really want to experience the kind of success that astounds? Then become a master at goals setting.

Here are several key areas to consider when planning your life's goals:

Self Development Goals

Occupational Goals

Spiritual Goals

Money/Income Goals

Standard of Living Goals

Family Goals

Volunteer Goals (service to others)

Take your time and consider each one separately. After you complete your goal setting exercise for each area, write one complete sentence summing up your overall desired result.

Read Them with Passion and Excitement

Next, keep a copy on your nightstand and read it each night before you go to bed. Recite your goals with passion. Close your eyes and see yourself succeeding.

Read them again with the same passion when you get up in the mornings.

Make this ritual your daily routine until it becomes a habit.

Finally, keep a succinct copy in your purse or wallet and read it occasionally throughout the day. And when things get tough as they surely will, read them over again and again until you get back in "the zone."

I wasted many years because I lacked a clear understanding of this science.

This daily ritual actually sets in motion what Dr. Robert Anthony (in his book entitled Advanced Formula for Total Success) calls the "law of attraction" which simply states, "Whatever you're looking for is looking for you."

No question, highly successful people, be they male or female, understand and employ this potent science.

Keep Moving Forward

As you know, your goals will forever be changing. Work on the ones that are most important at that time, but always keep an eye on the big prize.

Think about them all the time. Get emotional about achieving them. After you accomplish one, reward yourself, and then move on to the next one.

It won't be long before you've joined that small percentage of goal setters who have learned the secret to getting out of life exactly what they aim for.

So no more procrastinating...Get started this very minute. Right here right now.

"Nothing Becomes A Reality In Life Until It First Becomes Specific"

The Powerful Goals Setting Workshop

A dream realized begins with goals. No one becomes truly successful without first planning to do so.

Give serious thought to the following questions.

If you didn't have to worry about money to pay your bills, what would you do with your life? _____

_____

What makes you happy (occupation wise)? What would give you the greatest joy? _____

_____

What job could you get excited about going to every single morning? _____

_____

Take some time to really ponder these questions. You may discover this is what you're supposed to be doing with your life. In other words, your life's purpose.

Next set an overall goal for your life. In other words I want you to write your obituary. Here lies_____, he/she spent his/her life in service to others using his/her talents as a_____.

HOW TO CALL A MEETING WITH YOURSELF

Now write your overall goals for:

Finance (money). What will be your total lifetime (overall) net worth? (for retirement) $_____

    What will it be in 20 years? $_____

    In 10 years $_____

    In 5 years $_____

    In 1-4 years $_____

What will your yearly income look like?

    In 20 years $_____

    In 10 years $_____

    In 5 years $_____

    In 1-4 years $_____

What are your overall relationship goals? (marriage, # of children, etc.) _____

    In 20 years _____

    In 10 years _____

    In 5 years _____

    In 1-4 years _____

What are your overall spiritual goals? (read entire bible, teach bible school, learn to meditate) _____

    In 20 years _____

In 10 years _____

In 5 years _____

In 1-4 years _____

What are your overall educational goals? (PHD, JD, MBA, study abroad) _____

How far will you be in 20 years? _____

In 10 years _____

In 5 years _____

In 1-4 years _____

What are your overall personal goals? (Learn 3 languages, lose 30 pounds and stay in shape, read all of Shakespeare's work, etc.) _____

In 20 years _____

In 10 years _____

In 5 years _____

Next 1-4 years _____

Finally, what are your overall professional goals? (Head Ford Motor Co., start own business, sit on the Supreme Court)? _____

In 20 years _____

In 10 years _____

In 5 years _____

Next 1-4 years _____

Now take your yearly goals and break them down into quarterly, monthly, weekly, and daily to do goals.

You'll be amazed how far you'll come in a short period of time, and before you know it your dreams will become a reality. Remember, when you achieve one don't stop, immediately set another.

I'm not promising you that it's going to be easy, but I will promise you it'll be worth it.

We all know people who do nothing but talk. Every time you see them they're going to do something. They wear you out with talk. Run; don't walk from these kinds of people. They are toxic. They spend year after year "going to do something."

Still others are trying to live up to the dreams of their parents, their spouse or partner. But what about you? What about your dreams? It's time to go to work on your dreams.

Have You Lost Your Zest for Living?

Has your dream died? For many their dream is dead. They go to jobs they hate and do work that they despise. Well, it's time to get excited about life again.

Get up and go to work on your dreams. Go back to school, start your own business, take those exotic vacations.

It's not good enough to just wish and hope. You've got to make it happen for you and your family.

Art Williams said, (in his book All You Can Do Is All You Can Do), "People won't follow a bitter frustrated old crybaby." One who is carrying a big chip on their shoulder and who's mad at the world. No. People follow happy, excited, and positive people who exude confidence. You see everyone loves a winner.

Does that sound like you? Then you're on your way to stunning success. If you have a plan it won't be long before you reach the top.

If this doesn't sound like you, take immediate steps to change this pattern.

Use the success system found in this book to change the way you walk, talk, and think.

The principles found in this book will help you exude unstoppable confidence.

Folks, Dream again. Believe you can again. And work hard again. DREAM YOUR BIGGEST DREAM, and step into your future.

Day Three

On Day Three you will learn another powerful and exciting life skill that will stay with you the rest of your life. I can't wait to share it with you, so quick, turn the page and let's immediately put it to work for you...

Masters Goal Setters In Essence Create Their Own Future

> **Stunning Success Habit #2**
>
> Master the art of goals setting and spend time everyday in your dreams. Visualize (with emotion) the person you someday want to become, but act like that person now.

"Each And Every Day
Review Your Goals And Spend
Time In Your Dreams"

CHAPTER Eleven

DAY THREE

Invest Fifteen Minutes Today Bossing Your Thoughts.

The stunningly successful have learned a life skill that I find lacking among those who only wish for success.

It's ironic that the people who need it the most are the ones who employ it the least. Here it is...

They have learned to boss their thoughts.

They jealously protect the thoughts that enter their minds.

Their days are filled with reading, studying, and listening to other highly successful people and material. This provides them with a powerful shield of protection. And it's this type of protection that you'll need in order to sustain long term success.

I find it fascinating that most of them seldom listen to the car radio while driving to a meeting or appointment. Instead they choose to listen to motivational and skills development tapes.

Or, they take full advantage of that extra time they have to sharpen their delivery, master their techniques, and expand their knowledge.

If you want to succeed, you too must learn to control your thoughts.

Remember, do what others will not do or what others cannot do and you will be rewarded.

Develop an Appetite for Learning

You've heard the statement that readers are leaders. Learn this lesson and always take time to educate yourself. Develop an appetite for new learning.

Read, study, and continually absorb new information, so you'll be ready when your opportunity comes.

After all, success is simply being ready when your opportunity comes.

It's true; life will give you what you'll fight for, but you must continue to fight till your dream becomes a reality.

This brings us to the next life skill highly successful people employ:

The science of self-talk which goes hand-in-hand with bossing your thoughts.

I used to think that daily scheduled self-talk (or affirmations) was just a waste of time until I fully understood the power of the sub-conscience mind.

Control Your Thoughts/Control Your Life

The ability to control your thoughts is a crucial key to all the success you can ever desire. Follow me carefully on this.

Your sub-conscience mind, when directed to, will support whatever you truly believe. Wow, you need to read that again but this time read it slowly! Your sub-conscience mind, when directed to, will support whatever you truly believe.

Self-talk is simply the conversation you carry on with yourself all the time.

Everything you are is a by-product of what you've come to believe about yourself. And your beliefs, true or false, have become your reality.

Have you ever noticed people whom you may think are unattractive, but who exude enormous self-confidence?

While on the other hand, you may observe so-called beautiful people who lack the confidence to even walk in public?

The difference between the two is what they have come to believe about themselves. In other words how they think.

You Made You

Your self-image is the accumulation of attitudes, opinions, and thoughts you've stored up about yourself since childhood. All of these self proclamations combined with emotions have created a non-stop mental video that you've been recording for years. This recording controls how we think, act, and how we ultimately perform.

No matter what you feed your sub-conscience, it only serves to support you in your beliefs.

If you say, "I'm stupid," your sub-conscience mind makes an original recording and, every time you do something you've programmed as stupid, your sub-conscience mind reinforces that belief. It replays the tape and reinforces what you've said and replies, "Yes, you are stupid."

And get this, you're stuck with that original recording until you stop the tape, rewind, delete and reprogram it. The same holds true when you say, "I'm ugly, I'm dumb," or, "I'm a loser."

This is what I refer to as Mind Stamping™. It's like taking a rubber stamp and making an impression on a piece of paper, such as a bill stamped PAID.

Every Mind Stamp™ recording you make when declaring such statements serves to vigorously reinforce your belief over and over again, whether that belief is good or bad. In other words your sub-conscience says, "If you say you're stupid then you're stupid, after all you're the boss. I believe whatever you tell me, you're the master."

So you are the by-product of all your thoughts. As you think so are you.

Well it's time to get rid of that stinking thinking. How you ask? Keep reading…

You Can Change You

The good news is you can build a new successful self-image with your self-talk by using words that create mind pictures that in turn evoke strong emotions. Read it again slowly.

I know for some of you this is heavy stuff, but I assure you it works.

The use of self-talk and visualization techniques (Mind Stamping™ coming up in day four) will help create a whole new you.

Scripture says, *"As a man thinks so is he."* Now let's go back to your sub-conscience mind. It doesn't think in and of itself. That is your conscience mind. Your sub-conscience simply follows orders. Whatever orders you give it. Stay with me.

Now turn your thinking away from the negative to the positive. Declare that you're smart, and beautiful, or that you learn easily, and your sub-conscience mind will support you in that belief. It doesn't judge you one way or the other, it just obeys and supports.

DAY THREE *Invest Fifteen Minutes Today Bossing Your Thoughts.*

No Nonsense

This is some potent stuff and it may take you some time to fully appreciate and comprehend this science. This is not some wacky nonsense. Fact is you are employing this science this instance without even knowing it.

You are where you are today because you thought yourself there. Let me say that again. You are where you are today because you thought yourself there.

Every situation you find yourself in is a direct by-product of the thoughts you think.

Read the following poem by Walter D. Wintle and you'll get a better understanding of what I'm saying:

The Man Who Thinks He Can

If you **think** you are beaten, you are
If you **think** you dare not, you don't
If you like to win, but **think** you can't
It is almost certain you won't,

If you **think** you'll lose, you're lost
For out in the world we find,
Success begins with a fellow's will,
It's all in the state of the mind,

If you **think** you are outclassed you are,
You've got to **think** high to rise,
You've got to be sure of yourself before,
You can ever win a prize,

Life's battles don't always go
To the stronger or faster man,
But soon or late the man who wins

Is the man WHO **THINKS** HE CAN!

HOW TO CALL A MEETING WITH YOURSELF

It's true, thoughts become things. Think it long enough and believe it strong enough and it becomes your reality.

Chapter Twelve

Now Brace Yourself for this One...

This next statement is so powerful you'll have to read it over and over until it really sinks in. It's the reason self-talk is so effective when used with the visualization technique.

Are you ready for it?   Here it is...

Your sub-conscience mind doesn't know the difference between something that's simulated and something that really happens to you. Is it real or is it pretend? To the sub-conscience mind it makes no difference.

In other words you can actually program your mind to believing anything, whether it's true or false.

Those who are unsuccessful, unwittingly use this technique already. But what they end up programming is mostly negative thoughts and emotions.

Negative souls pronounce their limitations vigorously and declare how things cannot be accomplished. All they see is lack and want and don't understand how to break that cycle.

Well, the very same technique they already employ will produce positive results.

Daily self-talk helps you reprogram your sub-conscience mind, and make it believe you are the person you're striving to become, but that you are that person now. It's all in the mind.

Dr. Jack Addington called it psycho-genesis. Translated: psycho = mind, genesis = beginning. Everything begins in the mind.

Don't believe it? Try this exercise. Write a statement in your own handwriting declaring, "Today I am happy and I am strong." Read it once in the morning, once in the afternoon, and once just before going to sleep at night. As you dose off see yourself smiling and greeting people and see an image of yourself strong (whatever that means to you). Do this for five days and you'll notice the difference in your life. Remember, your word becomes law.

Talk Positive

Want to make this science work in all aspects of your life? Here's how.

Hold the vision (goals) of what you want long enough and back it up with strong emotional self-talk (everyday) and the results will astound you. In a short time even your friends will notice a stark difference in the new you.

Never Tolerate Berating - Even from Yourself

Let me ask you a powerful question. If you had a friend who talked to you the way you talk to yourself, how long would you keep him/her as a friend?

Stop attacking yourself and begin to build yourself up. If you don't, who will?

Here's the secret to effective self-talk, always recite your daily affirmations in the present tense. Such as:

I am in excellent health.

I learn and retain information easily.

I am excited about life and can't wait to get started each day.

I earn $100,000 a year.

I am totally confident in my skills and abilities.

Come up with some daily (in the moment) affirmations like the ones above which fit your current situation.

Now set aside some time in a quiet place, and see yourself doing, being, and experiencing all that you say. You've got to get emotional about your success. When you say, "I earn $100,000 a year," see and feel the money in your hand. That's a strong and powerful emotion combined with your self-talk.

Every person who experiences stunning success has learned the powerful technique of constructive self-talk.

Your keys to unthinkable wealth and riches lay in its mastery.

Spend time truly understanding this science. Study this science carefully.

Day Four

Wow! This Next One Will Blow You Away!

Have you heard of the highly effective technique called Focused Believing™?

Well, get ready because you're about to enter a whole new realm of discovery. Move quickly to Day Four and let the new you begin…

Boss Your Thoughts
And Everything Enters
The Realm Of Possibility

> **Stunning Success Habit #3**
>
> Invest 15 minutes today building yourself up with daily self-talk and thoroughly understand the science of training your sub-conscience mind.

DAY FOUR

Invest Fifteen Minutes Today On Focused Believing™.

Highly successful people have learned the art of what I call focused believing™. They never waiver in what they want.

They know along the way there'll be setbacks and disappointments, but they all have one powerful trait in common. They never give up!

They have this ability to stick it out through the toughest of times when others all around them quit.

Focused believing adds still another lethal weapon to your arsenal for success.

I developed this technique when I had problems believing I could speak before large groups of people, and I've used it ever since.

You know now, that before anything becomes a reality it first must be believable. And it all begins in your mind.

Everything you see with the naked eye started as a thought in someone's mind. And thoughts combined with pictures evoke strong emotions, which in turn produce stunning results.

This is how this technique was developed. As I struggled with believing I could succeed at speaking professionally before large groups of people, my mind went back to grade school.

Chapter Fourteen

One Lethal Weapon

I remembered as a child how my teacher encouraged us to look in magazines and cut out pictures of what we wanted to be. Some cut out pictures of doctors, some of firemen, and others of nurses.

This exercise was not only fun and exciting but also very powerful. So powerful I remember it to this day.

You see, it helped us focus our thoughts on what we wanted to become, not on our present circumstances. Many in my community didn't have much. I was the last of ten children. We didn't have an abundance of goods, but you know what? We truly believed we'd succeed. No one could tell us any different. We had this child-like faith.

What Do You Mean?

What I mean by that is, you can tell a child back in June that you will get him a bicycle for Christmas.

Once that child has a vision of the goal (that bicycle), no one but no one can change that child's mind. The parents may be struggling to pay the bills, but that child expects to get that bicycle regardless.

The child believes it so strongly that he starts giving out rides to his little friends (in June) even though Christmas is a long six months away.

You see, in his mind he already has the bike. Don't believe it? Let one of his little friends make him angry and he'll say, "I'm not going to let you ride my bike when I get it for Christmas."

Now, all of this is happening and there is no physical evidence of a bicycle at all. All he has is a picture of what he wants. It's in the child's mind and nothing is going to change that.

It'll Work Now

Well, I reasoned if it worked then, it will work now. I could hardly contain my excitement as I recalled how powerful this exercise is.

I immediately started thumbing through magazines. What was I looking for? I was looking for a picture of a person (any person) speaking at a convention.

My Search Yielded Fruit

After about two hours of searching, I found it. A picture of a person speaking in front of about three thousand people. My excitement was almost unbearable.

I now had a picture that supported my goal of becoming a professional speaker. A picture I could focus on to help remove all doubts about my ability to speak before large groups of people.

The Exciting Next Step

Here's what I did. I took a picture of myself and placed it over the face of the speaker in the picture. This was a very powerful moment in my life. Now, the vision was made plain for me. It became crystal clear.

I knew from that very moment on my dream would become a reality. I cannot stress enough the potency of this simple technique I call Focused Believing™.

I believe the reason most people fail is not because they're not smart enough, or because they lack the skills necessary to win.

What You See Is What You'll Be

No, most people fail because they simply cannot picture themselves being successful at whatever it is they want out of life. Well, what you see is what you'll be.

I heard the story of a lady who was overweight her whole life. She struggled to keep her weight under control. It hurt her to look in the mirror, so she placed mirrors where she could only see her face.

She never went anywhere, or did anything, till one day a friend asked her what was her goal concerning her weight. Armed with that information the lady's friend then asked her for a picture (of herself).

Her friend searched diligently and found a picture of another woman at about the size her overweight girlfriend wanted to be. Then she glued her girlfriend's picture on top, and took it to her.

The lady wept, and wept, and wept. You see, for the first time she could see herself being the size she really wanted to be. Within months she accomplished her goal and became the woman in the picture.

I tried it for myself and it worked for me as well.

If you can see it you can be it.

It Really Can Happen

Your goals, combined with pictures, backed up with daily self-talk and heartfelt emotions are your power potion for stunning success.

You've got to actually see yourself doing and being the person in the picture.

Spend just fifteen minutes a day on this exercise and experience the results for yourself. Five minutes in the mornings, five minutes in the evenings, and five minutes whenever you think about it during the day. The results will be startling and will stun the people around you. Try it for whatever you want in life, a new car, a new house, a new you.

But please remember you must always be the person in the picture.

It Really Works

Well guess what, within one year of initiating this technique, I was speaking professionally in front of thousands of people.

It happened just as I pictured it, with only one exception. It was a thousand times better than I'd ever expected.

It's Better Than You Expect

And so it is with success. When you reach your goals, it's always better than you've ever imagined.

Remember that success is not a destination, but a journey. A journey up the yellow brick road, where you'll encounter people like the cowardly lion who appears brave on the outside, but is really afraid to take the journey with you.

You'll encounter well-meaning people who'll go part of the way, but just don't have the heart to finish. What good is a start without a finish?

Never Give Up

They'll demand that you turn back at every dark corner and every creepy sound saying it's for your own good.

They'll come in the form of friends who say you're not brave enough, co-workers who say you're not smart enough and family members who say you're not sharp enough. But keep on your journey.

There'll be times when your days are so long, they'll seem endless. And your nights so dark you'll think the day will never break. But keep on your journey.

The winds will blow and the clouds will hang low.

On the road to success you'll encounter wicked naysayers who'll try to discourage you all along the way. But keep on your journey.

Yes, success will test you to the limit, to see if you really want what you say you want. Whatever you do, whatever you feel, whatever you see, and whatever negative you hear, just keep on your journey.

After Awhile The Sun Will Shine Again

And soon enough, if you walk far enough, if you sing long enough, and if you stand tall enough, the light will shine upon your path.

The clouds will roll back, the winds will cease, and the beautiful warm sun will shine on your face.

Make sure you keep your eyes open, because help will come from many unlikely sources.

Perhaps a scarecrow, whose outer appearance will be deceiving, but inside, beats the heart of a champion. One who'll stick with you when everyone else quits.

Cherish the one who sticks with you, for you won't find very many on this road called success. But, every once in awhile you'll find a traveler.

Oh, by the time you get to the success palace, you'd probably have made a whole new set of friends. Friends who believe in you and support you when all others quit.

Dream Big Dreams

So dream big dreams. Set goals for your life that are bigger than anything you could do on your own. There is magic in thinking big. Go ahead, because dreams do come true.

You'll find that the doors to stunning success will swing wide open to the man and woman whose mind is trained, whose will is unbroken, and whose purpose is sure.

Who are these people? They are the winners, the select few who have mastered the principles outlined in this book. They are the ones who experience stunning success.

After all, success (winning) is a learned habit just like all other habits such as smoking, swimming, and riding a bike. You too can be a constant success.

Are you game? Then make this book a study in how to make a habit of succeeding.

Are You Ready for Day Five?

This next one will make the hairs on the back of your neck stand up. Get ready to build Unstoppable Self-Confidence. Hurry, flip the page now...

*When You're Absolutely Sure You
Want Success, Your Success Is
Absolutely Sure*

> **Stunning Success Habit #4**
>
> Spend 15 minutes today using the technique called Focused Believing™. Cut pictures from magazines and like a child believe your dreams will come true.

"Your goals, combined with pictures, backed up with daily self-talk and heartfelt emotions are your power potion for stunning success."

DAY FIVE

Invest Fifteen Minutes Building Your Self Confidence

No doubt you've noticed the stunningly successful exude an aura of total self-confidence. If it was sweat it would run out their pores.

They smile, walk faster, and talk louder. They're winners and you can spot them easily even in a crowd.

Confidence comes from knowing. Knowing yourself, knowing your purpose, and knowing your abilities.

People who lack self-confidence are confused about their place in life.

On the other hand, successful people are constantly expanding their knowledge. They are ever searching for what succeeds and why.

We live in the information age and those with superior knowledge and the understanding of how to market that knowledge will win big in this new economy. That's just the way it is.

The More You Learn the More You Earn

It's a fact that as your educational level expands so does your income. Now education doesn't necessarily mean going to a formal school, although I strongly encourage it. Education simply means you're motivated to gather all the necessary information to win at the game you're playing.

There's the game of law, medicine, football, golf, stocks, finance, real estate, etc. You've got to know "your stuff."

Let me encourage those of you who think you're passed the age you feel you can learn; it's never too late.

And to young people who feel that when they graduate from high school or college, that's the end of the learning process. That they're finished, and that's all the education they'll need.

Wrong. Wrong. Dead wrong. You're not finished, not by a long shot. Your journey has just begun.

How to Stay On Top

Listen carefully; your ability to stay on the cutting edge of information in your chosen field, by keeping abreast of current trends, will always be a key to your success now and throughout your career.

Take note of the stunningly successful and you'll find they're the ones called on to deal with the burning issues of today and they're the ones highly sought out for their answers. Be it technology, medicine, business, politics or military.

They are the movers and shakers. People who get things done. Why? Because they are in the know. They have superior knowledge of their subject matter and will always do a little bit more than the others in their field to win.

Why Managers Make More

True enough, everyone wants to be recognized as a person who "knows their stuff," but few are willing to study hard and pay the price it takes to be that person.

This is the very reason the stunningly successful exude such a high degree of self-confidence.

They do what others don't want to do and people flock to them in numbers.

Take Tiger Woods; pro golfer, he spends more time on the practice links than any other golfer. In fact he has caused golfers all over the world to sharpen their game.

People flock to him in numbers. Including those who don't even play golf.

Why? Because everyone loves winner and wants to know how they acquired such unstoppable self-confidence. People who are not self-motivated will always pay a portion of their income to managers and supervisors who motivate them.

In other words the managers and supervisors do what other workers will not do. So, the less self-motivated you are, the more of your income you give up pure and simple. According to the very best sources, the average person uses only 10% of their mental capacity.

But there's good news. You can stack the odds in your favor.

Be Honest With Yourself

How? By taking an honest look at how you spend your time each day.

By now, you realize that every thing, good or bad, starts in the mind.

So today, take a note pad and keep track of what influences your thinking.

What do you...?

- Watch on Television?

- Listen to on the Radio?

- Read and digest from newspapers and magazines?

- What type of music do you listen to?

- What type of programs are you drawn to?

- What type of people do you associate with?

- Who do you spend time talking to on the phone?

Whether you realize it or not, all of these entities influence the way you think. They either help build or help destroy your self-confidence.

Call A Meeting With Yourself

If you really want to get a clear picture of yourself, follow yourself around for an entire week. Take notes, and at the end of the week, call a meeting with yourself. Lay all the cards on the table and do an honest assessment.

What you see may not be pretty and may even shock you, but remember you can reprogram your mind for stunning success.

How Do I Change?

Here's how to change those self-defeating habits and start on the road to stunning success.

Immediately begin to …

Limit your intake of negative thoughts.

Chose programs on television that build or at least don't destroy your positive self-image and positive thinking.

If you can't find any positive programs on the radio during your drive time, turn it off. It's better to be with your own positive thoughts than to be with others' negative ones.

Don't be afraid to invest in motivational cassette/CD's programs that build your self-confidence and expand your educational knowledge.

There are plenty of good books on tape that you can listen to while you drive. You'll see a marked improvement in your knowledge.

Get rid of toxic people and toxic relationships that tear you down instead of build you up. I know we all want friends and want to be liked, but if those so-called friends are not supporting you in where you're going, ask yourself, "Are they really my friends?"

Post positive reinforcement signs and posters in strategic places such as, your bedroom, your office, in your wallet, and any other places where you can see them. This will help to keep your mind focused and it'll stir daily excitement.

Read, read, read. Read everything you can that builds you up. Keep it simple. You don't have to read a novel sized book everyday. Often a daily word, a chapter or verse will do. Just keep reading to reinforce your positive beliefs. And finally...

Those who experience stunning success have learned the art of winning friends and influencing people. (And it has nothing to do with money).

They...

- Wear a smile on their face.

- Wear a smile in their voice.

- Make Friends of everyone.

- They reach out to others.

- They remember peoples' names, which is the sweetest sound anyone can hear.

- Give others the benefit of the doubt.

- Build up but never tear down.

- Get truly interested in the other person.

- Become great listeners.

Start with these simple steps and you are on your way to unthinkable health, wealth, and happiness.

Chapter Seventeen

One Rich Man

The richest person I've personally met never made a million dollars in one year.

He didn't have a different automobile to drive every day of the week.

His home wasn't a mansion, but a single-family track home.

No, he never made millions, but he was extremely rich. He was rich in the keys of life...

He wore a smile that could melt a glacier. He respected your name by remembering it and calling it with dignity and class. And no matter whose company he was in (and he was often in the company of some very successful people), he made you feel special.

By watching him, I learned some powerful lessons about success that I'll never forget.

He never met a stranger, and never acted strange when you met him. You felt blessed just to be in his presence.

Although he wore expensive suits, he never looked down his nose at others and never missed an opportunity to speak an encouraging word.

I know it sounds like something out of a movie, but my friend enriched me by enriching others. This I witnessed with my own eyes.

Everyone should be blessed to meet such a person. He was the richest person I ever met and I'll never forget him.

Don't Step On Others

Success is nothing if you step on others to get it. You don't have to beat others down to build yourself up.

On the contrary, I've found it's the people who build up others that radiate and exude total self-confidence.

They don't have this public success but private failure. They are truly happy beings who are constantly enriching others. They are beams of light in a very dark world.

> They have unstoppable self-confidence.
> Build Others' Self Confidence And You'll Never
> Have To Worry About Your Own

Stunning Success Habit #5

Spend 15 minutes today building your self-confidence using the techniques in this chapter and remember when you help build others' confidence you are really building your own.

Well, It's Decision Time!

Folks, think back to those High School pep rallies. The excitement, the fun, and the thrill of just being alive.

Well, it's time to get excited about life again. Life will give you what you'll fight for.

Dust off your dreams, get up and go to work on them. Go back to school, start that business, take that trip, buy that house.

It's not good enough to just wish and hope. Do something about it.

Folks, Dream again. Believe you can again. And work hard again.

DREAM YOUR BIGGEST DREAM, and step into your future.

Declare boldly, " I'M WORKING ON MY DREAMS™!"

DREAMS DO COME TRUE.   I know...I'm sharing mine with you.

Now go out there and...

MAKE YOUR DREAMS KING™!

"Make Your Dreams King™"

Meeting Adjourned!

So there you have it. You now have all the tools you'll need to produce stunning success in your own life.

To Recap this Meeting With Yourself

- Find your true purpose in life! Do what makes you whole (Day One)

- Dream big dreams and be specific about what you want and where you're going! (Day Two)

- Seize control of what goes in your mind and what comes out your mouth! (Day Three)

- Make the vision (of what you expect) plain by using the technique called Focused Believing™ cutting pictures from magazines and placing your picture on top. Be that person! (Day Four)

- Know "your stuff." This gives you unstoppable self-confidence. Serve others with your talents and be the very best at what you do for a living and your success is absolutely sure! (Day Five)

This being all...

Meeting Adjourned!

About The Author

Dubbed *"King Of Inspiration"*

Cubie Davis King is the founder and President of Inspiration University and Chief Executive Officer of Gold Crown Enterprises, Inc. with headquarters in San Diego, CA.

Born in the projects of east Dallas, he has spent his life studying successful people and the science of how they succeed. He has voluntarily lent his teaching skills and knowledge inspiring inner-city youth through the Junior Achievement Program.

Mr. King is a Viet Nam era veteran, former Federal Contracts Negotiator and executive with Xerox Corp. He is also a former Senior Vice President for sales with Citigroup. Now travel the country as a professional speaker.

Mr. King received his B.B.A and went on to complete his M.B.A from National University in San Diego, CA. He is an international author, publisher, and speaker. With an uncanny ability to captivate the hearts and minds of audiences, he is sought out by professional groups and organizations the world over. He blends his passion for speaking with real life experiences, thereby captivating his audiences with excitement and energy.

To Reach Mr. King:

Gold Crown Enterprises, Inc.
7046 Broadway #356
Lemon Grove, Ca 91945

www.goldcrowninc.com

1-800-483-1255

Notes

Notes